WHO AM I?

THE TEACHINGS of SRI RAMANA MAHARSHI

Copyright © 2020 Sanage Publishing House LLP

All rights reserved. No part of this publication may be reproduced, distributed, or transmitted in any form or by any means, including photocopying, recording, or other eletronic or mechanical methods, without the prior written permission of the publisher, except in the case of brief quotations embodied in critical reviews and certain other noncommercial uses permitted by copyright law. For permission requests, write to the publisher, addressed "Attention Permissions Coordinator," at the address below.

Paperback: 978-939156001-0

Any references to historical events, real people, or real places are used fictitiously. Names, characters, and places are products of the author's imagination.

Sanage Publishing House LLP
Mumbai, India

sanagepublishing@gmail.com

Ramana Maharshi (30 December 1879 – 14 April 1950) was an Indian Hindu sage. He is widely thought of as one of the most outstanding Indian spiritual leaders of recent times. Having attained enlightenment at the age of 16, he was drawn to the holy mountain of Arunachala in southern India, and remained there for the rest of his life. Attracted by his stillness, quietness and teachings, thousands sought his guidance on issues ranging from the nature of God to daily life.

CONTENTS

Introduction 5

Who Am I? Nan Yar 9

Introduction

Who am I? is the title given to a set of questions and answers bearing on Self-enquiry. The questions were put to Bhagavan Sri Ramana Maharshi by Sri M. Sivaprakasam Pillai, about the year 1902. Sri Pillai, a graduate in philosophy, was at the time employed in the Revenue Department of the South Arcot Collectorate. During his visit to Tiruvannamalai in 1902 on official work, he went to Virupaksha Cave on Arunachala Hill and met the Maharshi there. He sought from him spiritual guidance and solicited answers to questions relating to Self-enquiry. As Bhagavan was not talking then, not because of any vow he had taken but because he did not have the inclination to talk, he answered questions put to him by writing. As recollected and recorded by Sri Sivaprakasam Pillai, there were thirteen questions and answers to them given by Bhagavan. This record was first published by Sri Pillai in 1923 (in the original Tamil), along with a couple of poems composed by himself relating how Bhagavan's grace operated in his case by dispelling his doubts and by saving him from a crisis in life.

Who am I? has been published several times subsequently.

The present rendering is of the text in the form of twenty-eight questions and answers.

Along with *Vicharasangraham (Self- Enquiry)*, *Nan Yar* (Who am I?) constitutes the first set of instructions in the Master's own words. These two are the only prose pieces among Bhagavan's works. They clearly set forth the central teaching that the direct path to liberation is Self-enquiry. The particular mode in which the enquiry is to be made is lucidly set forth in *Nan Yar*. The mind consists of thoughts. The "I"-thought is the first to arise in the mind. When the enquiry "Who am I?" is persistently pursued, all other thoughts get destroyed, and finally the "I"-thought itself vanishes leaving the supreme non-dual Self alone. The false identification of the Self with the phenomena of non-self such as the body and mind, thus ends, and there is illumination, sakshatkara. The process of enquiry, of course, is not an easy one. As one enquires "Who am I?", other thoughts will arise; but as these arise, one should not yield to them by following them; on the contrary, one should ask, "To whom do they arise?" In order to do this, one has to be extremely vigilant. Through constant enquiry one should make the mind stay in its source, without allowing it to wander away and get lost in the mazes of thought created by itself. All other disciplines such as breath-control and meditation on the forms of God should be regarded as auxiliary practices. They are useful so far as they help the mind to become quiescent and one-pointed. For the mind that has gained skill in concentration Self-enquiry becomes comparatively easy. It is by ceaseless enquiry that the thoughts are destroyed and the Self realised – the plenary Reality in which there is not even the "I"-thought, the experience which is referred to as "Silence".

This, in substance, is Bhagavan Sri Ramana Maharshi's teachings in *Nan Yar* (Who am I?).

T.M.P. Mahadevan
University of Madras
June 30, 1982

BHAGAVAN SRI RAMANA MAHARSHI
(At the age of 21)

Who Am I?
Nan Yar

All living beings desire to be happy always, without any misery. In everyone there is observed supreme love for oneself. And happiness alone is the cause of love. In order therefore, to gain that happiness which is one's nature and which is experienced in the state of deep sleep, where there is no mind, one should know oneself. To achieve this, the Path of Knowledge, the enquiry in the form of "Who am I?", is the principal means.

1. Who am I?

The gross body which is composed of the seven humours (dhatus), I am not; the five cognitive sense organs, viz., the senses of hearing, touch, sight, taste and smell, which apprehend their respective objects, viz. sound, touch, colour, taste and odour, I am not; the five cognative sense organs, viz., the organs of speech, locomotion, grasping, excretion and procreation, which have as their respective functions, speaking, moving, grasping, excreting and enjoying, I am not; the five vital airs, prana, etc., which perform respectively the five functions of inbreathing, etc., I am not; even the mind which thinks, I am not; the nescience too, which is endowed only with the residual impressions of objects and in which there are no objects and no functionings, I am not.

2. *If I am none of these, then who am I?*

After negating all of the above mentioned as 'not this', 'not this', that Awareness which alone remains – that I am.

3. *What is the nature of Awareness?*

The nature of Awareness is Existence- Consciousness- Bliss.

4. *When will the realization of the Self be gained?*

When the world which is what-is-seen has been removed, there will be realization of the Self which is the seer.

5. Will there not be realization of the Self even while the world is there (taken as real)?

There will not be.

6. Why?

The seer and the object seen are like the rope and the snake. Just as the knowledge of the rope which is the substratum will not arise unless the false knowledge of the illusory serpent goes, so the realization of the Self which is the substratum will not be gained unless the belief that the world is real is removed.

7. When will the world which is the object seen be removed?

When the mind, which is the cause of all cognition and of all actions, becomes quiescent, the world will disappear.

8. What is the nature of the mind?

What is called 'mind' is a wondrous power residing in the Self. It causes all thoughts to arise. Apart from thoughts, there is no such thing as mind. Therefore, thought is the nature of mind. Apart from thoughts, there is no independent entity called the world. In deep sleep there are no thoughts, and there is no world. In the states of waking and dream, there are thoughts, and there is a world also. Just as the spider emits the thread (of the web) out of itself and again withdraws it into itself, likewise the mind projects the world out of itself and again resolves it into itself. When the mind comes out of the Self, the world appears. Therefore, when the world appears (to be real), the Self does not appear; and when the Self appears (shines) the world does not appear. When one persistently inquires into the nature of the mind, the mind will end leaving the Self (as the residue). What is referred to as the Self is the Atman. The mind always exists only in dependence on something gross; it cannot stay alone. It is the mind that is called the subtle body or the soul (jiva).

9. What is the path of inquiry for understanding the nature of the mind?

That which rises as 'I' in this body is the mind. If one inquires as to where in the body the thought 'I' rises first, one would discover that it rises in the heart. That is the place of the mind's origin. Even if one thinks constantly 'I-I', one will be led to that place. Of all the thoughts that arise in the mind, the 'I'-thought is the first. It is only after the rise of this that the other thoughts arise. It is after the appearance of the first personal pronoun that the second and third personal pronouns appear; without the first personal pronoun there will not be the second and third.

10. How will the mind become quiescent?

By the inquiry 'Who am I?'. The thought 'Who am I?' will destroy all other thoughts, and like the stick used for stirring the burning pyre, it will itself in the end get destroyed. Then, there will arise Self-realization.

11. What is the means for constantly holding on to the thought 'Who am I?'

When other thoughts arise, one should not pursue them, but should inquire: 'To whom do they arise?' It does not matter how many thoughts arise. As each thought arises, one should inquire with diligence, 'To whom has this thought arisen?'. The answer that would emerge would be 'to me'. Thereupon if one inquires 'Who am I?', the mind will go back to its source; and the thought that arose will become quiescent. With repeated practice in this manner, the mind will develop the skill to stay in its source. When the mind that is subtle goes out through the brain and the sense-organs, the gross names and forms appear; when it stays in the heart, the names and forms disappear. Not letting the mind go out, but retaining it in the Heart is what is called 'inwardness' (antarmukha). Letting the mind go out of the Heart is known as 'externalisation' (bahirmukha). Thus, when the mind stays in the Heart, the 'I' which is the source of all thoughts will go, and the Self which ever exists will shine. Whatever one does, one should do without the egoity 'I'. If one acts in that way, all will appear as of the nature of Siva (God).

12. Are there no other means for making the mind quiescent?

Other than inquiry, there are no adequate means. If through other means it is sought to control the mind, the mind will appear to be controlled, but will again go forth. Through the control of breath also, the mind will become quiescent; but it will be quiescent only so long as the breath remains controlled, and when the breath resumes the mind also will again start moving and will wander as impelled by residual impressions. The source is the same for both mind and breath. Thought, indeed, is the nature of the mind. The thought 'I' is the first thought of the mind; and that is egoity. It is from that whence egoity originates that breath also originates. Therefore, when the mind becomes quiescent, the breath is controlled, and when the breath is controlled the mind becomes quiescent. But in deep sleep, although the mind becomes quiescent, the breath does not stop. This is because of the will of God, so that the body may be preserved and other people may not be under the impression that it is dead. In the state of waking and in samadhi, when the mind becomes quiescent the breath is controlled. Breath is the gross form of mind. Till the time of death, the mind keeps breath in the body; and when the body dies, the mind takes the breath along with it. Therefore, the exercise of breath control is only an aid for rendering the mind quiescent (*manonigraha*); it will not destroy the mind (*manonasa*).

Like the practice of breath control, meditation on the forms of God, repetition of mantras, restriction on food, etc., are but aids for rendering the mind quiescent.

Through meditation on the forms of God and through repetition of mantras, the mind becomes one-pointed. The mind will always be wandering. Just as when a chain is given to an elephant to hold in its trunk it will go along grasping the chain and nothing else, so also when the mind is occupied with a name or form it will grasp that alone. When the mind expands in the form of countless thoughts, each thought becomes weak; but as thoughts get resolved the mind becomes one-pointed and strong; for such a mind Self-inquiry will become easy. Of all the restrictive rules, that relating to the taking of sattvic food in moderate quantities is the best; by observing this rule, the sattvic quality of mind will increase, and that will be helpful to Self-inquiry.

13. The residual impressions (thoughts) of objects appear unending like the waves of an ocean. When will all of them get destroyed?

As the meditation on the Self rises higher and higher, the thoughts will get destroyed.

14. Is it possible for the residual impressions of objects that come from beginningless time, as it were, to be resolved, and for one to remain as the pure Self?

Without yielding to the doubt 'Is it possible, or not?', one should persistently hold on to the meditation on the Self. Even if one be a great sinner, one should not worry and weep 'O! I am a sinner, how can I be saved?' One should completely renounce the thought 'I am a sinner' and concentrate keenly on meditation on the Self; then, one would surely succeed. There are not two minds – one good and the other evil; the mind is only one. It is the residual impressions that are of two kinds – auspicious and inauspicious. When the mind is under the influence of auspicious impressions it is called good; and when it is under the influence of inauspicious impressions it is regarded as evil.

The mind should not be allowed to wander towards worldly objects and what concerns other people. However bad other people may be, one should bear no hatred for them. Both desire and hatred should be eschewed. All that one gives to others one gives to one's self. If this truth is understood who will not give to others? When one's self arises all arises; when one's self becomes quiescent all becomes quiescent. To the extent we behave with humility, to that extent there will result good. If the mind is rendered quiescent, one may live anywhere.

15. How long should inquiry be practised?

As long as there are impressions of objects in the mind, so long the inquiry 'Who am I?' is required. As thoughts arise they should be destroyed then and there in the very place of their origin, through inquiry. If one resorts to contemplation of the Self unintermittently, until the Self is gained, that alone would do. As long as there are enemies within the fortress, they will continue to sally forth; if they are destroyed as they emerge, the fortress will fall into our hands.

16. What is the nature of the Self?

What exists in truth is the Self alone. The world, the individual soul and God are appearances in it, like silver in mother-of-pearl; these three appear at the same time and disappear at the same time.

The Self is that where there is absolutely no 'I'-thought. That is called 'Silence'. The Self itself is the world; the Self itself is 'I'; the Self itself is God; all is Siva, the Self.

17. Is not everything the work of God?

Without desire, resolve, or effort, the sun rises; and in its mere presence, the sun-stone emits fire, the lotus blooms, water evaporates, people perform their various functions and then rest. Just as in the presence of the magnet the needle moves, it is by virtue of the mere presence of God that the souls governed by the three (cosmic) functions or the fivefold divine activity perform their actions and then rest, in accordance with their respective *karmas*. God has no resolve; no *karma* attaches itself to Him. That is like worldly actions not affecting the sun, or like the merits and demerits of the other four elements not affecting all-pervading space.

18. *Of the devotees, who is the greatest?*

He who gives himself up to the Self that is God is the most excellent devotee. Giving one's self up to God means remaining constantly in the Self without giving room for the rise of any thoughts other than that of the Self.

Whatever burdens are thrown on God, He bears them. Since the supreme power of God makes all things move, why should we, without submitting ourselves to it, constantly worry ourselves with thoughts as to what should be done and how, and what should not be done and how not? We know that the train carries all loads, so after getting on it why should we carry our small luggage on our head to our discomfort, instead of putting it down in the train and feeling at ease?

19. What is non-attachment?

As thoughts arise, destroying them utterly without any residue in the very place of their origin is non-attachment. Just as the pearl-diver ties a stone to his waist, sinks to the bottom of the sea and there takes the pearls, so each one of us should be endowed with non-attachment, dive within oneself and obtain the Self-Pearl.

20. Is it not possible for God and the Guru to effect the liberation of a soul?

God and the Guru will only show the way to liberation; they will not by themselves take the soul to the state of liberation.

In truth, God and the Guru are not different. Just as the prey which has fallen into the jaws of a tiger has no escape, so those who have come within the ambit of the Guru's gracious look will be saved by the Guru and will not get lost; yet, each one should, by his own effort pursue the path shown by God or Guru and gain liberation. One can know oneself only with one's own eye of knowledge, and not with somebody else's. Does he who is Rama require the help of a mirror to know that he is Rama?

21. Is it necessary for one who longs for liberation to inquire into the nature of categories (tattvas)?

Just as one who wants to throw away garbage has no need to analyse it and see what it is, so one who wants to know the Self has no need to count the number of categories or inquire into their characteristics; what he has to do is to reject altogether the categories that hide the Self. The world should be considered like a dream.

22. Is there no difference between waking and dream?

Waking is long and dream short; other than this there is no difference. Just as waking happenings seem real while awake, so do those in a dream while dreaming. In dream the mind takes on another body. In both waking and dream states thoughts, names and forms occur simultaneously.

23. Is it any use reading books for those who long

for liberation?

All the texts say that in order to gain liberation one should render the mind quiescent; therefore their conclusive teaching is that the mind should be rendered quiescent; once this has been understood there is no need for endless reading. In order to quieten the mind one has only to inquire within oneself what one's Self is; how could this search be done in books? One should know one's Self with one's own eye of wisdom. The Self is within the five sheaths; but books are outside them. Since the Self has to be inquired into by discarding the five sheaths, it is futile to search for it in books. There will come a time when one will have to forget all that one has learned.

24. What is happiness?

Happiness is the very nature of the Self; happiness and the Self are not different. There is no happiness in any object of the world. We imagine through our ignorance that we derive happiness from objects. When the mind goes out, it experiences misery. In truth, when its desires are fulfilled, it returns to its own place and enjoys the happiness that is the Self. Similarly, in the states of sleep, samadhi and fainting, and when the object desired is obtained or the object disliked is removed, the mind becomes inward-turned, and enjoys pure Self-Happiness. Thus the mind moves without rest alternately going out of the Self and returning to it. Under the tree the shade is pleasant; out in the open the heat is scorching. A person who has been going about in the sun feels cool when he reaches the shade. Someone who keeps on going from the shade into the sun and then back into the shade is a fool. A wise man stays permanently in the shade. Similarly, the mind of the one who knows the truth does not leave Brahman. The mind of the ignorant, on the contrary, revolves in the world, feeling miserable, and for a little time returns to *Brahman* to experience happiness. In fact, what is called the world is only thought. When the world disappears, i.e., when there is no thought, the mind experiences happiness; and when the world appears, it goes through misery.

25. *What is wisdom-insight (jnana drishti)?*

Remaining quiet is what is called wisdom-insight. To remain quiet is to resolve the mind in the Self. Telepathy, knowing past, present and future happenings and clairvoyance do not constitute wisdom- insight.

26. What is the relation between desirelessness and wisdom?

Desirelessness is wisdom. The two are not different; they are the same. Desirelessness is refraining from turning the mind towards any object. Wisdom means the appearance of no object. In other words, not seeking what is other than the Self is detachment or desirelessness; not leaving the Self is wisdom.

27. What is the difference between inquiry and meditation?

Inquiry consists in retaining the mind in the Self. Meditation consists in thinking that one's self is Brahman, Existence- Consciousness-Bliss.

28. What is liberation?

Inquiring into the nature of one's self that is in bondage, and realising one's true nature is liberation.

LIST OF TITLES WITH ISBN NO.

ISBN	TITLE
9788194914129	1984
9789390575220	1984 & Animal Farm (2In1)
9789390575572	1984 & Animal Farm (2In1): The International Best-Selling Classics
9789390575848	35 Sonnets
9789390575329	A Clergyman's Daughter
9789390575923	A Study In Scarlet
9789390896097	A Tale Of Two Cities
9789390896837	Abide in Christ
9789390896202	Abraham Lincoln
9789390896912	Absolute Surrender
9789390896608	African American Classic Collection
9789390575305	Aldous Huxley: The Collected Works
9789390896141	An Autobiography of M. K. Gandhi
9789390575886	Animal Farm
9789390575619	Animal Farm & The Great Gatsby (2In1)
9789390575626	Animal Farm & We
9789390896158	Anna Karenina
9789390575534	Antic Hay
9789390896165	Antony & Cleopatra
9789390896172	As I Lay Dying
9789390896226	As You like it
9789390575671	At Your Command
9789390575350	Awakened Imagination
9789390575114	Be What You Wish
9789390896233	Believe In yourself
9789390896998	Best of Charles Darwin: The Origin of Species & Autobiography
9789390896684	Best Of Horror : Dracula And Frankenstein
9789390575503	Best Of Mark Twain (The Adventures of Tom Sawyer AND The Adventures of Huckleberry Finn)
9789390896769	Black History Collection
9789390575756	Brave New World, Animal Farm & 1984 (3in1)

ISBN	Title
9789390896240	Brother Karamzov
9789390575053	Bulleh Shah Poetry
9789390575725	Burmese Days
9789390896257	Bushido
9789390896066	Can't Hurt Me
9788194914112	Chanakya Neeti: With The Complete Sutras
9789390896042	Crime and Punishment
9789390575527	Crome Yellow
9789390575046	Down and Out in Paris and London
9789390896844	Dracula
9789390575442	Emersons Essays: The Complete First & Second Series (Self-Reliance & Other Essays)
9789390575749	Emma
9789390575817	Essential Tozer Collection - The Pursuit of God & The Purpose of Man
9789390896578	Fascism What It Is and How to Fight It
9789390575688	Feeling is the Secret
9789390575190	Five Lessons
9789390575954	Frankenstein
9789390575237	Franz Kafka: Collected Works
9789390575282	Franz Kafka: Short Stories
9789390575060	George Orwell Collected Works
9789390575077	George Orwell Essays
9789390575213	George Orwell Poems
9788194914150	Greatest Poetry Ever Written Vol 1
9788194914143	Greatest Poetry Ever Written Vol 1
9789390896301	Gulliver's Travel
9789390575961	Gunaho Ka Devta
9789390575893	H. P. Lovecraft Selected Stories Vol 1
9789390575978	H. P. Lovecraft Selected Stories Vol 2
9789390896059	Hamlet
9789390575022	His Last Bow: Some Reminiscences of Sherlock Holmes
9789390896134	History of Western Philosophy
9789390575121	Homage To Catalonia

9789390896219	How to develop self-confidence and Improve public Speaking
9789390896295	How to enjoy your life and your Job
9789390575633	How to own your own mind
9789390896318	How to read Human Nature
9789390896325	How to sell your way through the life
9789390896370	How to use the laws of mind
9789390896387	How to use the power of prayer
9789390896028	How to win friends & Influence People
9788194824176	How To Win Friends and Influence People
9789390896103	Humility The Beauty of Holiness
9789390896653	Imperialism the Highest Stage of Capitalism
9789390575084	In Our Time
9789390575169	In Our Time & Three Stories and Ten poems
9789390575145	James Allen: The Collected Works
9789390896189	Jesus Himself
9789390575480	Jo's Boys
9789390896394	Julius Caesar
9789390575404	Keep the Aspidistra Flying
9789390896400	Kidnapped
9789390896424	King Lear
9789390575824	Lady Susan
9789390896455	Law of Success
9789390896264	Lincoln The Unknown
9789390575565	Little Men
9789390575640	Little Women
9788194914174	Lost Horizon
9789390896462	Macbeth
9789390896929	Man Eaters of Kumaon
9789390896523	Man The Dwelling Place of God
9789390896349	Man The Dwelling Place of God
9789390575909	Mansfield Park
9788194914136	Manto Ki 25 Sarvshreshth Kahaniya
9789390896509	Marxism, Anarchism, Communism
9789390575664	Mathematical Principles of Natural Philosophy

ISBN	Title
9788194914198	Meditations
9789390575800	Mein Kampf
9789390575794	Memory How To Develop, Train, And Use It
9789390896486	Mind Power
9789390896585	Money
9789390575039	Mortal Coils
9789390575770	My Life and Work
9789390896035	Narrative of the Life of Frederick Douglass
9789390575152	Neville Goddard: The Collected Works
9789390575985	Northanger Abbey
9789390896530	Notes From Underground
9789390896547	Oliver Twist
9789390575459	On War
9789390575541	One, None and a Hundred Thousand
9789390896554	Othelo
9789390575435	Out Of This World
9789390575015	Persuasion
9789390575510	Prayer The Art Of Believing
9789390575091	Pride and Prejudice
9789390896561	Psychic Perception
9789390575381	Rabindranath Tagore - 5 Best Short Stories Vol 2
9789390575367	Rabindranath Tagore - Short Stories (Masters Collections Including The Childs Return)
9789390575374	Rabindranath Tagore 5 Best Short Stories Vol 1 (Including The Childs Return
9789390896622	Romeo & Juliet
9789390896127	Sanatana Dharma
9789390575596	Seedtime & Harvest
9789390896639	Selected Stories of Guy De Maupassant
9789390575206	Self-Reliance & Other Essays
9789390575176	Sense and Sensibility
9789390575299	Shyamchi Aai
9789390896738	Socialism Utopian and Scientific
9789390896646	Success Through a Positive Mental Attitude
9789390575428	The Adventures of Huckleberry Finn

ISBN	Title
9789390575183	The Adventures of Sherlock Holmes
9789390575343	The Adventures of Tom Sawyer
9789390896691	The Alchemy Of Happiness
9789390575862	The Art Of Public Speaking
9789390896288	The Autobiography Of Charles Darwin
9788194914181	The Best of Franz Kafka: The Metamorphosis & The Trial
9789390575008	The Call Of Cthulhu and Other Weird Tales
9789390575107	The Case-Book of Sherlock Holmes
9789390896110	The Castle Of Otranto
9789390896745	The Communist Manifesto
9789390575589	The Complete Fiction of H. P. Lovecraft
9789390575497	The Complete Works of Florence Scovel Shinn
9789390896820	The Conquest of Breard
9789390896813	The Diary of a Young Girl
9789390896332	The Diary of a Young Girl The Definitive Edition of the Worlds Most Famous Diary
9789390575701	The Great Gatsby, Animal Farm & 1984 (3In1)
9789390575312	The Greatest Works Of George Orwell (5 Books) Including 1984 & Non-Fiction
9789390575992	The Hound of Baskervilles
9789390896707	The Idiot
9789390896714	The Invisible Man
9789390575657	The Knowledge of the holy
9789390575558	The Law & the Promise
9789390896721	The Law Of Attraction
9789390896776	The Leader in you
9789390896363	The Life of Christ
9789390896196	The Man-Eating Leopard of Rudraprayag
9789390896783	The Master Key to Riches
9789390575268	The Memoirs Of Sherlock Holmes
9789390896479	The Midsummer Night's Dream
9789390575466	The Mill On The Floss
9789390896790	The Miracles of your mind
9789390896660	The Mutual Aid A Factor in Evolution
9789390896448	The Origin of Species

ISBN	Title
9789390896905	The Peter Kropotkin Anthology The Conquest of Bread & Mutual Aid A Factor of Evolution
9789390896806	The Picture of Dorian Gray
9789390896271	The Picture of Dorian Gray
9789390575275	The Power Of Awareness
9789390896356	The Power of Concentration
9788194824169	The Power of Positive Thinking
9789390575411	The Power of the Spoken Word
9788194914105	The Power Of Your Subconscious Mind
9789390896899	The Power of Your Subconscious Mind
9789390896417	The Principles of Communism
9789390575787	The Psychology Of Mans Possible Evolution
9789390896615	The Psychology of Salesmanship
9789390575732	The Pursuit of God
9789390575398	The Pursuit of Happiness
9789390896851	The Quick and Easy Way to effective Speaking
9789390575947	The Return Of Sherlock Holmes
9789390575138	The Road To Wigan Pier
9789390896981	The Root of the Righteous
9789390575855	The Science Of Being Well
9788194914167	The Science Of Getting Rich, The Science Of Being Great & The Science Of Being Well (3In1)
9789390896011	The Screwtape Letters
9789390896073	The Screwtape Letters
9789390575336	The Secret Door to Success
9789390575695	The Secret Of Imagining
9789390896868	The Secret Of Success
9789390896431	The Seven Last Words
9789390575930	The Sign of the Four
9789390896004	The Sonnets
9789390896516	The Souls of Black Folk
9789390896875	The Sound and The Fury
9789390575244	The State and Revolution
9789390896882	The Story of My Life
9789390896936	The Story Of Oriental Philosophy

ISBN	Title
9789390896752	The Strange Case of Dr. Jekyll and Mr. Hyde
9789390896943	The Tempest
9789390575916	The Valley Of Fear
9789390575879	The Wind in the willows
9789390896080	The Wind in the willows
9789390575763	Their eyes were watching gofd
9789390575831	Three Stories
9789390896950	Twelfth Night
9789390896592	Twelve Years a Slave
9789390896677	Up from Slavery
9789390896974	Value Price and Profit
9789390896967	Wake Up and Live
9789390896493	With Christ in the School of Prayer
9789390575602	Your Faith is Your Fortune
9789390575473	Your Infinite Power To Be Rich
9789390575251	Your Word is Your Wand
9789390575718	Youth
9789391316099	A Christmas Carol
9789391316105	A Doll's House
9789391316501	A Passage to India
9789391316709	A Portrait of the Artist as a Young Man
9789391316112	A Tale of Two Cities
9789391316747	A Tear and a Smile
9789391316167	Agnes Gray
9789391316174	Alice's Adventures in Wonderland
9789391316136	Anandamath
9789391316181	Anne Of Green Gables
9789391316754	Anthem
9789391316198	Around The World in 80 Days
9789391316013	As A Man Thinketh
9789391316242	Autobiography of a Yogi
9789391316266	Beyond Good and Evil
9789391316761	Bleak House
9789391316778	Chitra, a Play in One Act
9789391316310	David Copperfield

ISBN	Title
9789391316075	Demian
9789391316785	Dubliners
9789391316051	Favourite Tales from the Arabian Nights
9789391316235	Gitanjali
9789391316068	Gravity
9789391316150	Great Speeches of Abraham Lincoln
9789391316662	Guerilla Warfare
9789391316839	Kim
9789391316822	Mother
9789391316211	My Childhood
9789391316846	Nationalism
9789391316327	Oliver Twist
9789391316853	Pygmalion
9789391316334	Relativity: The Special and the General Theory
9789391316389	Scientific Healing Affirmation
9789391316341	Sons and Lovers
9789391316587	Tales from India
9789391316372	Tess of The D'Urbervilles
9789391316396	The Awakening and Selected Stories
9789391316402	The Bhagvad Gita
9789391316303	The Book of Enoch
9789391316228	The Canterville Ghost
9789391316907	The Dynamic Laws of Prosperity
9789391316006	The Great Gatsby
9789391316860	The Hungry Stones and Other Stories
9789391316433	The Idiot
9789391316440	The Importance of Being Earnest
9789391316297	The Light of Asia
9789391316914	The Madman His Parables and Poems
9789391316457	The Odyssey
9789391316921	The Picture of Dorian Gray
9789391316464	The Prince
9789391316938	The Prophet
9789391316945	The Republic
9789391316518	The Scarlet Letter

ISBN	Title
9789391316143	The Seven Laws of Teaching
9789391316525	The Story of My Experiments with Truth
9789391316532	The Tales of the Mother Goose
9789391316549	The Thirty Nine Steps
9789391316594	The Time Machine
9789391316600	The Turn of the Screw
9789391316983	The Upanishads
9789391316617	The Yellow Wallpaper
9789391316426	The Yoga Sutras of Patanjali
9789391316990	Ulysses
9789391316624	Utopia
9789391316679	Vanity Fair
9789391316020	What Is To Be Done
9789391316686	Within A Budding Grove
9789391316693	Women in Love